NETiquette (On-Line Etiquette)

Tips for Adults & Teens:
Facebook, MySpace, Twitter!
Terminology….and More

By Michelle Cimino

PublishAmerica
Baltimore

First printing

PublishAmerica has allowed this work to remain exactly as the author intended, verbatim, without editorial input.

ISBN: 978-1-61582-317-8
PUBLISHED BY PUBLISHAMERICA, LLLP
www.publishamerica.com
Baltimore

Printed in the United States of America

NETiquette (On-Line Etiquette)

Tips for Adults & Teens:
Facebook, MySpace, Twitter!
Terminology….and More

Preface

When I first started exploring the social networking sites I soon realized, in my opinion, some sites are mostly used to talk about cute guys and the next big party (MySpace). Ok, that's cool, I used to call on the phone, but hey, that was quite a few years ago. Once I finally dug in and *really* started exploring the chat sites I read a conversation….it was a skinny dipping story that quickly became x-rated. Whoa! Talk about details. I felt like I was reading a smut novel—I was embarrassed to be reading it, but I couldn't stop either! Yet that was exactly what I knew I should do—stop reading! I immediately made my younger daughter cancel her MySpace account. After all, she was only 12 at the time, which forced me to realize she was too young for MySpace. Duh. Just for the record, I finished reading the story. I know, sick.

Now if I was the skinny dipper (which at my age would not be a good idea unless it was very dark, the moon was covered by clouds and I had on my panty hose) I still don't think I would share all the details. At least I don't think I would want to share that kind of information with my ALL my friends, and definitely not complete strangers. Some adventures are supposed to be experienced, not shared. Anyhoo…I read and kept reading and then remembered I wasn't the only person reading. These kids were pretty young, I could tell by the language, and it scared the crap out of me. Other people started to comment and I left the site soon after. I'm not sure how much of the story was true, but the content was very graphic. So either way, it was embarrassing.

Of course my daughter re-assured me that she wasn't messing around on chat sites, but I had happened upon the site accidently myself and knew how easy that would be for her as well. I didn't change my mind and she cancelled her account. It's almost like allowing her to go to an R rated movie. How can a parent control these kinds of things? How can we protect our kids? Shoot, how can I protect MYSELF! Don't get me wrong, I'm not one of those super protective parents that are completely suppressing my children with extreme measures. But I do worry about protecting them from some stuff that they need a little more maturity to handle. That experience freaked me out a little (Ok a lot) and I didn't want her to feel the same way.

Now, just to confuse you even more, I have to mention the good stuff too. It's truly amazing the stuff that can happen within these social sites. Example: the kindness of strangers. I've seen many people on LinkedIn and Twitter help people get jobs. Usually people they barely know or complete strangers for that matter. The networking ability of these sites can be truly helpful. No kidding! People tell someone, then they tell someone and they tell someone (remember that old hair commercial?).

How about the dating sites? Their totally romantic commercials make me believe that love can be found on-line. I'm still a firm believer in the power of a person's voice or the chemistry of meeting a person face to face. Fact is, this is how people date now. How many times have you heard someone say *it's better than meeting in a bar*? My husband and I joke about putting ourselves on the dating sites just to see if they would match us up together. Wouldn't that be sad if they didn't? I mean, we've been married twenty years now. It would be a fun experiment if I wasn't a big fat chicken.

I didn't realize that when I wrote my first book, "Cell Phone Etiquette, observations from a Mom" that it was just the beginning. Looking back, I realize that when I bought my teenage daughter her first phone, it was not just the ability to call someone or text her buddies, but it was her gateway to the ENTIRE world. Let me explain. At the time, I knew that my daughter's cell phone meant everything to her. She had begged us for months and wouldn't let up until we finally gave in. Now, years later, I realize that her phone is her connection to the outside world. Not only does she communicate with us (her parents), her friends in her close circle, but also friends and family far away. I had no idea that a person could update a status, search for phone numbers or upload photos and videos from their cell phone *to* all the social networking sites!! In return, receive updates *from* social sites to their cell phones. I had no idea what we were getting ourselves into! It was then that I realized we all need a little *NETIQUETTE*. I wish I could take credit for that word, but nope, I read it somewhere.

Chapter 1

First Things First

There are a gazillion networking sites out there. I did not research ALL of them, but a few of the most popular. My first piece of advice: Before you dive in head first to any networking site, I recommend you **CHECK IT OUT** thoroughly. Spend some time wondering around and getting to know it. Look into the safety features and age limits. Get a 'feel' for the site and compare it to your personality. You can always quit if the fit doesn't seem right, so you don't have to fear commitment! I recommend you do the same if you kid mentions an interest in a site. Check it out. See if you feel they are ready to dive into the world wide web! It can be scary but it can be fun too!

Twitter is a site for micro-blogging (blogging means typing whatever you want for others to see—kind of like a text message of sorts). Twitter prompts you by asking the question *what are you doing?* What ever you choose to type about may or may not be important to other people. This site enables its users to send and read other users' updates known as tweets. Tweets are posts of up to 140 characters total. People tweet what they are cooking for dinner all the way to Ellen DeGeneres' tweets about her daily show content. I've also heard recently that news stories are appearing on Twitter before they are appearing on Television. People are choosing to tweet information opposed to calling their local news station. You name it, you can hear about it (and comment on it) on Twitter.

Remember the War of the Worlds? What's keeping that from happening on these social networks? Scary! I can just imagine someone blogging about an alien attack and all the rest of us falling for it. If a creative person made it believable I would probably fall for it. Don't get any ideas! Twitter allows you to 'follow' people that interest you and people that you interest will follow you. You can search for people or topics that you are interested in. Finding things that interest you is a good place to start. A nice 'jumping off' point.

Facebook is a social networking website that users can join organized by city, workplace, school and/or region to connect and interact with other people. It is a great way to keep in touch with your 508 friends you've never met (my tongue is in my cheek right now, in case you were wondering). Facebook also provides a prompt *what's on your mind?* Seems to me this age group is pretty wide. Middle School, High School, College (big time) all the way to a few of my stay-at-home/working moms and even my Mother-In-Law (how cool is she?). Facebook started when Mark Zucerberg and his roommates (Dustin Moskovitz and Chris Hughes) decided to put the paper face books at Harvard University on the computer. I'm no Harvard alumni, but I guess Harvard used to print information about their campus community and give this book out to incoming students, faculty and staff as a way to get to know other people on campus. Pretty cool to know how that started, huh? They have age limit of 13 and over. You can upload pictures and videos and share them. You have to 'accept' friends in order for them to view your home page and ask to be friends with other people in order to view their page.

MySpace still seems pretty young to me, according to the things they talk about, but hey, I could be wrong. Their social networking website has an interactive, user-submitted network of friends, personal profiles, blogs, groups, photos, music and videos for teenagers and adults internationally. You can customize your home page with graphics, pictures and all kinds of cartoons and stuff that appeal to a both a young and old crowd.

Okay, I have to admit, the first time I went on **Twitter** was for research for this book. So I'm even going to try to pretend to be an expert. I do think that being a newbie at this sort of thing is exactly what you probably are (or you might not be reading this book), so we're even! Back to my story, at first, I was curious about the whole 140 character thing. Is our attention span so short now that what we have to say needs to be condensed? I typed in Twitter into my browser and it came right up, as expected. Then I proceeded to watch their cute little video about what Twitter was. Did you know you can get Twitter updates directly to your cell phone? Cool. Then, I decided to sign up. I made up a user name, a password (accepted after two tries) and uploaded my photo. Then what? I didn't know! A few stories came up that looked like "news" updates. So I read a few of those. Then I was kicked out. "Twitter was over capacity, too many tweets, please wait a moment and try again later". Ok. That was my experience.

I let it rest for a few days and tried again. I tweeted a few things and felt like I was talking to myself. Which I do all the time, so I don't know why it was freaking me out now. Could it be because I was *typing* to myself when usually I *talk*? (Don't act like you don't know what I'm talking about). Even though it felt a little funny, I kept at it. I knew the world was buzzing about Twitter and how cool it was, so I was determined to figure what all the fuss was about.

At first, I felt like 140 characters definitely is not enough for me! I'm a writer for goodness sake! I need pages and pages! In addition, nothing exciting happens to me on a daily basis that I feel is Twitter worthy anyway. Then it got exciting! I searched a few things that interested me (wouldn't you like to know what they were). I dove into a couple of conversations that were happening at the moment (it's all real-time, you know) and I felt like I connected. I recommend trying that and seeing what you think. I did find myself more drawn to the people that actually used words and not cryptic sentences. It was too much work trying to decipher the tweet to understand their meaning. Maybe that could be another piece to this whole etiquette thing, hint to users: just say it!

My ego did get a boost when I got an alert that Brittany Spears was following me. I would be a fool to think the *real* Brittany was following me, why would she? It did make me giggle though and sit up a little straighter in my seat.

I was listening to my favorite radio station the other day. It's kind of an alternative station with music that will make your ears bleed if you turn it up just so….(I know, weird, but I really do like it). Anyway, the radio posted a tweet to announce the magic song name that would get you free tickets to a concert. All you were supposed to do was follow them (the radio station), they give you the song name on Twitter, and then when you hear the song played on the radio, you call in. I wouldn't have thought to twitter the radio station for that kind of information. Those of us that don't twitter would have been left out of the loop. Interesting.

On all these sites you can Lurk, Follow, Block, Tweet, Trail, Spiral, and a number of other things you need a dictionary for. Of course, I've added that in the back of the book. Caution: some terminology might not be appropriate for your kids. However I got the information from kids so your kids probably already know them anyway! Sorry, just keepin' it real.

Chapter 2

Safety Measures: Be Safe for Goodness Sake

Of course, I would be remiss if I didn't add a chapter on safety precautions. We have all heard the scary stories of on-line predators. Creepers meeting kids and doing God-knows-what to them without their parents knowing they were meeting a stranger. People posting pictures that do permanent damage to their future and the future of others. News stories are cropping up all the time that some police agencies are pressing charges for naked pictures found on kid's cell phones. They are pressing *criminal* charges. These kids will have to register as a sex offender. We are talking about young teenage kids here! That should look great on their job application later. So here are some tips:

1) **PASSWORD:** First of all, never give your password to anyone. You should change your password at least every 6-12 weeks. If you think that your password has been compromised, change it immediately. Your password should be very hard for anyone to guess. Try using combinations of upper and lower case letters, numbers and symbols. Don't write it down where others will have access to it.

2) **PERSONAL INFO**: Never give out your full name, address, school, town where you live, where you work, e-mail address and phone numbers. Things like where you hang out every day after school should never be mentioned. Nothing that could lead a bad guy to you.

3) **REPORT**: Always tell someone (parent, co-worker or social site reporting area) about any threatening messages, tweets or posts that you receive. Harassment and hate speech is just un-cool. Don't allow them to get away with it, and don't allow it to happen to you or anyone you know. You deserve better. And I won't think you're a tattle tail.

4) **BE CAREFUL**: Responding to users you don't know in real life. There are people out there who aren't really who they say they are. Be careful what you say and how much information you disclose. Also, be careful what questions you answer on a survey, and what survey's you take. These survey's range from issues on drinking, drugs to other questionable topics. It's pretty easy to see how this could lead to potential danger. If you like meeting people from all over the world, that's fine. Be careful if they want to meet in person. Arrange to meet in a public place and DON'T go alone. Seriously, this means you! **Note to parents**: your kid mentions to you that they want to meet with someone they met on-line, don't judge! Don't freak-out! Be happy they told you. It is the wave of the future. You should offer to go with them.

5) **NEVER**: Lie about your age. Be as honest as possible on these sites without compromising your safety. Even though Twitter says they are not directed towards people under the age of 18, they don't ask for your age when setting up an account. Facebook says you have to be 13 to join. But my younger

daughter lied about her age to get on MySpace (big trouble young lady!). She knew how to do the math. So if you are too young to join, there is a reason. Waiting isn't that hard and it's good practice for the real world—and the rest of your life. Anything you have to wait for is usually worth the wait.

6) **SEARCH RESULTS**: Most sites give you the ability to turn off your public visibility. What if you are a teacher who doesn't want their High School students knowing about their personal life? This might not be the case for you, but you might have other reasons for choosing this option (escape convict). Remember though that this will remove you from search results, making it hard for people to find you. Most sites offer some customization in this area.

Scammers/Pedophiles/Creepers are very smart people. Be smart in return. I wish these guys would channel their incredible brains into getting a legitimate job. Great websites, like the following, offer more safety information for parents.

Netsmartz.org
SafeTeens.com
Webwisekids.org
BlogSafety.com
CommonSenseMedia.com

Chapter 3

We All Need a Little Privacy…Settings

Another piece of advice: Understand **PRIVACY.** I've found it a little tough for me to keep my site split between personal and business. So I recommend you understand the privacy settings that are available and you learn how to use them. Most sites are defaulted to 'public' for all to see. Changing these settings right away is a good idea. By doing so your profile becomes private and only approved people can see your updates.

Something that I have done: I have put my contacts into groups (more details below). Some people fall into 'business friends' or 'family' or 'general friends'. Some people over lap. This has been working out for me so far. My husband uses Facebook for business only. So he has a hard time when he gets a friend request that isn't related to business. So he has done the same with his groupings. This will save you some embarrassment in the long run when your girlfriend's college age kids post pictures of their last drunken party that show up on your wall! (This comment was not meant for any of MY perfect friends, in case you are reading this!). If you use the privacy features well, you might even be able to accept your boss's friend request.

Twitter: You can change who sees your Twitter messages and updates by selecting "protect my updates' box in the 'settings' area. You can also control whose updates you receive, when you receive them and in what device you get these updates (cell phone or web).

MySpace: After you login, scroll to the bottom of your page. On the left hand side you will see 'privacy policy' scroll to 'privacy settings'. You will have options regarding who your profile is viewable by:

1. everyone
2. everyone 18 & older
3. my friends only

Facebook: Allows you to create private groupings of friends based on your personal preference. No, I don't mean gay or lesbian, black or white (I guess you could of course). I mean you can create a 'friend list' for Business, Friends (social) and or Family. These are just examples, but seem to be the most popular. Each list then can have specific privacy policies set to them. For example, you might want friends to see pictures from the party you were at last night, but you don't want 'business' or 'family' contacts to see them. You can configure your friends groups by visiting the 'friend's area' on your Facebook page.

I've heard more and more that large companies and even some colleges are checking these social networks for additional information on their applicants. Not the kind of stuff you would put on your college application or your resume'. But only the interesting stuff you put 'out there' for the world to see. The *real* you. I guess if you put it out there, you are willing to take the risk of WHO will see it. Parents are watching, friends of parents are watching. Bosses and co-workers are watching. Now colleges and employers are watching. Watch out! I know how hard it is for young people to think about their future. But this stuff is out there forever. **BE SMART WHAT YOU POST.**

When I talk to teenagers about us parents 'watching', they say we are spying. Spying is to observe secretly. Like putting on a black mask and dark clothing and looking through binoculars. If all I have to do is pull up your public page, its like reading the newspaper. You put it out there…how can I be spying? I'm not reading your locked diary. Now, what I consider to be acceptable might not be to other people and vice versa. That is why the internet and social sites are so controversial. It's a conversation starter I'll tell ya that much!

Chapter 4

Old Friends, New Friends, Everybody Needs Friends

How many times has this happened to you? You haven't seen someone for 20 years or forgot they even existed then boom, you get a friend request? You add them as a friend and never hear from them again. I know it's a sad story. I have been very choosy with my friend requests. I only request those I really want to stay in contact with. Of course, there are the occasional people that I don't remember very well, then you stress out about 'what if I don't accept' them? Then the drama sets in. Welcome to my world! If I don't recognize a name or face I don't add them. Period. However, I am totally UNCOOL. Just ask my kids. I'm told it's a contest or at least a quest to get the most friends. I didn't know!

I have found the re-connecting to people I haven't seen in a very long time can be awesome. Pictures of their husband, kids last vacation, etc. But if they ask me to be their friend and I never hear from them again I'm sad. Boo Hoo. I'm not interested in being part of their "how many friends can I get" scheme.

Of course, now that I've completed my research for this book, I realize that I am a Facebook Mom. I thought that I was cool, but really the kids think I'm spying on them, my nieces and nephews HAD to accept me as a friend or become the black sheep of the family, and I actually asked some of my daughter's friends to be friends with me. I'm so completely pathetic and totally un-cool. So now you know. Wanna be my friend?

So **DO NOT**: add anyone as a friend unless you really want to be friends! I don't know about you, but I'm not a marble. I'm a person, not something you collect! This aspect of socializing really shouldn't be a contest about popularity. Everyone who is on these social sites knows that you can't possibly know all these people. It's all for show. Be nice. It's absolutely impossible to stay in touch with 508 friends anyway, so why would you want to? These sites can be majorly cool if used properly. It's nice to wish a person Happy Birthday when without the social site I wouldn't have known it was their Birthday at all. Makes me look good—sweet!

Also, **DO NOT**: add people you don't even know! Why would you do this? I guess if you think their picture is hot or something….but then that's weird. Still, I stick to my original advice, do not add people you don't know. I'm not saying that everyone on the internet is a pedophile or stalker, but you never know! Be careful and choosey. I know many people casually, but I thought the entire idea of social networking is to keep in touch with people I am really interested in. It saves me a phone call! Some people accept every invite and then complain about all the people inviting them—it's your own fault! You made your bed, now you know what to do!

I know that teens and young adults use these sites specifically to MEET new people. I get it. I really do. I just want all of them to be careful. It seems to me that the word reputation doesn't mean anything anymore. I mean, I'm not one to really base my life on what other's think of me, but that attitude took me years to acquire. I knew I was supposed to be the girl you could bring home to mama—even though I did stupid things. I'm also not saying that if Facebook came out when I was seventeen I wouldn't be a complete idiot, because I know I would have been. That's why I'm writing this book! To help all you idiots out there! JK! But seriously, I also know that being 'Bad' is the cool thing. Every girl I see wants to be sexy. All the dudes want to be studs. Ok fine. I wanted to be bad and mysterious when I was growing up too. But millions of people weren't watching then either.

Just a quick shout out to all my nieces and nephews….thanks for accepting my friend request even though you probably didn't want to or felt like you had to. Maybe you have some security settings already in place for me. Good for you! I haven't seen anything bad, and I wouldn't tell your parents if I did. So thanks for being nice to me!

Chapter 5

Social Network Mail or Personal E-Mail?

I remember back years ago when I got my first e-mail account. I was so excited that I e-mailed a bunch of friends to let them know I was finally connected! The response I got back wasn't so great. I thought by putting my entire message in capital letters it would save me time. I can't tell you how many people e-mailed me back asking: WHY ARE YOU YELLING AT ME??? Oops! I didn't know that all caps meant yelling. That rule still stands today. So...**DON'T** send a message in all cap's unless you're yelling.

There are so many ways to get in touch with people these days; it's hard to decide which way to go. Do I send a regular 'ol e-mail? Do I Facebook them? Should I text them on their phone? Twitter? Do I write a letter (what's that? I know—nobody gets snail mail anymore! Teens don't even know the price of a stamp—I'm not kidding, I've asked a bunch of them just to check.)

When I first signed up on Facebook, I kinda liked the fact that my personal e-mail would notify me that I had a message on Facebook. My personal e-mail is sent to my cell phone….so, when I had time I could log on to Facebook and check out my messages and respond.

However, the flip side of this coin: sometimes I'm messing around on my computer, (when I'm supposed to be folding laundry) and get an alert that I have a personal e-mail. So I log on to my personal e-mail only to find out that I have to log onto Facebook to respond to their message. Geez. That is a drag. So….I can see how this would irritate some people. Need a solution?

E-MAIL RULE: If you have someone's personal e-mail, use that first! You can always mention it again on their social site if you want to later. It also works well to ask people "what is the best way to reach you?" Seems silly I know, but some people spend hours each day on Facebook, but don't read their personal e-mail messages for weeks.

As for receiving notifications, I check my personal e-mails every day (sometimes twice) and Facebook about once a week. I don't want to get sucked in, so I pace myself. So the only advice I can give you is to play around little to figure out the perfect way for you. You might even find you're logging on to your favorite social site and not using personal e-mail anymore. Some of my friends have already done this.

Chapter 6

A Picture Is Worth a Thousand Words

This is a goody! Where do I begin? Let's start with the basics. When you first sign up on any social network one of the first things they ask for is a picture. This will be used for your profile picture. This will be what people will see when they are searching for you. Please **DO NOT**: upload a picture of your cat/dog, wish-you-were-her-supermodel, favorite actor/actress or your car. In case you were wondering I was trying to find you! There were 5,000 John Smith's and I didn't know which one to invite because it had a picture of a 'sunset' instead of your cute little mug. How sweet and beautiful....but it wasn't you. I don't care if you snap a quick picture with your cell phone while brushing your teeth and submit that one. At least it will do until you can go to Glamour Shots and get a fancy make-over.

Please be sure to put A picture in there! I can't tell you how many people I've looked up and never invited because all they had was the Social Site's default logo. The name was right, the school seemed right, right city, but no picture. Come on, you take a Driver's License picture right? It can't be worse than that!

WARNING! Be careful! On-line social networks are not a storage facility for your priceless photographs. All of your priceless photos need to be protected at home. **DO NOT** upload all your photos thinking they will be there forever. Huge websites can crash just like your home computer will. So, please save your originals.

I would also like to say that I DO enjoy looking at your photographs. However, 125 photos of your son's soccer game is a little much. I know he plays soccer; I know you are very proud. **PLEASE DO:** submit a few of the BEST photos. I want to see them, I really do, but too many photos makes me want to pull my hair out. I've been on MySpace viewing a site that had too many videos and pictures and it caused my computer to fry. I think this problem has been corrected, but I'm afraid to visit their page again.

On another serious note, please **DO NOT:** submit nasty, naked or drunken pictures of yourself or anyone you know or don't know. It's not nice! It's embarrassing and can affect people's lives for many, many years to come. So far there isn't any law that states you have to get permission to post pictures you have in your hot little camera (or cell). That's the beauty of the net. There are a few photos of me in other people's albums and it seems I'm always holding a cocktail. Now that I look like an alcoholic, I'm just thrilled they can post these without asking me first. So, you better hope you don't have any old pictures at your ex-girlfriends that she can post of you! You can protect what is posted on your site, but you have no control over what other people post of you on their site.

I know there are people going around party hopping snapping pictures of people. That will, without a doubt, be posted tomorrow. Remember Michael Phelps? Ouch! Yes, it can happen to you too. Maybe not as many people will care like they did about Michael Phelps, but it could ruin your future just the same. Or at worst embarrass you, or cause you to loose your job.

There is a way for you to share photos with people that are actually 'in' the photos. Maybe that would be a good rule of thumb: **PLEASE DO**: share your photos, but only with the people who are IN the photos. And if the picture does not cast them in the best light, perhaps you can ask first. Then, if they see the need to post them for the entire universe to see, power to the people! I know that some kids think this is hilarious to post these terrible pictures. Karma man! It's going to come back and bite you in the butt one of these days. I warned you.

In Facebook under 'profile privacy' you can modify these news feeds. Under 'customize' you can select who sees pictures posted to your wall.

Also, the act of notifying another person that they are in a photo, or identifying people in your photo is called **Tagging**. You can accomplish this by going to the photo page and selecting 'My Photos'. Click the 'Edit Album' link. Click on the person's face in the photo and then select their name in the box that pops up. If their name is not in the box, you can type it in the text field. If you need to tag yourself, select 'me'. Repeat this process (over and over—to completely annoy all your friends and family) for everyone in the photo that you would like to tag. Click 'Save Changes' and you have just TAGGED someone! Cool, huh?

Remember, that when you tag a person in a photo, it will be accessible from the 'View Photos of' link under their profile picture. You can also Tag people while looking at other people's photos. Meaning, I can be looking through another persons photos (browsing) and see someone I know. I can then tag this photo with their name so everyone knows that I know and now they know it's them! (Got it? Did that make sense at all?)

Another scary thing: if YOU didn't upload the photo that you are tagged in, you cannot remove or edit the tag. Only the owner of the photo and the tagged user will be able to do so. Another words, you can remove the tag from your page, but it doesn't stop the photo from going out to everyone else announcing it's you with pie on your face.

The only TAGGING I can relate to was chasing the boys around the playground in the first grade. We would tag them saying "You're It!" I believe this is the same idea in a way. By tagging someone in a photo it's like a pretend tap on the shoulder saying "Everyone look at them!" Life was much easier back then, and I wasn't (usually) doing anything I was particularly ashamed of. I would try and kiss the boys. By the way, I pretty fast back then....Yep, I did a lot of kissing. But guess what, no pictures of it! HA!

Chapter 7

Private Conversation vs. Airing Your Dirty Laundry

It seems that every generation has bad things to say about the next up-and-coming generation. That's not what I'm here to do. I don't think the next generation is a bad one….just different. When I was a kid and I told a secret to my best friend, I really prayed that she wouldn't tell anyone. I mean it—I wanted her to keep my secret! I wanted to share, but not with every Tom, Dick and Harry. Through out my life I've had friends that were good at keeping secrets and some that weren't. This new generation is putting ALL their secrets, thoughts, hopes, dreams, experiences and pictures (good and bad, appropriate and un-appropriate) out there for the entire World to experience with them. I'm not saying that's a bad thing, just hard for me to relate to. I try to keep my mistakes my secret. You guys share everything! Shouldn't you be choosy about WHAT you share?

Today, Boyfriends/girlfriends aren't 'official' until it's posted on their social network of choice (Facebook, MySpace, etc). How funny. Back in my day, we would just show up somewhere holding hands and it was official. Of course, I had already called my closest friends and let them in on the news, so they made sure to pass it on. Back then, three-way-calling was the bomb. I guess the social sites are the same thing….only now I automatically get notification of this kind of news along with every single person you ever thought to know. It is a very quick way to 'spread the word' to everyone, I'll admit. It's better than a hickey.

After interviewing a few people about their 'X's' on some sites, they mentioned the heartbreak involved at still having the 'connection' to their x's site. They tell me they can't help wanting to check-in and see what's new after they have broken up. New boy/girl friends are posted or pictures of some great party that they didn't get invited to. There are ways to block these people. I wouldn't recommend blocking anybody unless they are a creeper. However, save your heart some pain; don't go visiting any old boy/girl friend sites until your heart heals. Why put yourself through that? Give yourself some time, and check in later when you're stronger and have moved on yourself. If its any consolation, your X is checking your site too, I guarantee it.

Another funny phenomenon is the 'Vultures'. These are the people that as soon as a status changes to 'single' the vultures come out. The 'friend' that wants to let you know they are available to console you during your heartache. Yeah, right! They are just waiting to pounce on you while you're vulnerable. Sounds like a bunch of my old boyfriends.

Please **DO NOT** ask someone out in front of the world! Geez, what if they say no? It's awkward enough to try to meet people, don't set yourself up. See them in person, like you actually care, and ask them out then. That way, if they turn you down, you don't have to post some terrible lie about how you didn't really want to go out with them. How it was just a dare or something.

Please **DO NOT**: break up with someone on your social site. I really don't want to read about your last fight or the latest gossip that you are spreading. Geez, some things are private. Go see your boy/girl friend in PERSON and tell them how you feel. Don't post it on the wall! Brutal! Have a heart will ya? This is another one of those karma things, I'm telling ya, what goes around comes around.

I spoke with another teen who recently cancelled his MySpace account because of the 'drama'. When I pressed further to find out exactly what he meant, he proceeded to share with me that during his MySpace time he had a girlfriend. This information was obvious on his site. He also had other pictures of himself with friends, etc. Another girl posted comments about how 'sexy' his pictures were. His girlfriend got mad and jealous. How was he supposed to control what other people said about his pictures?

He also mentioned the fact that MySpace has 'top friends' lists. His friends that weren't listed at 'top friends' would get their feelings hurt. He decided to escape. Now he only conducts communications on his cell phone or in person. He claims his level of drama has dropped considerably and he hasn't missed being a part of a social site for one minute.

DO NOT talk trash about your boss/supervisor/co-worker! Hello? Are you crazy? You never know who reads that stuff and/or passes it on. If you don't think your boss/supervisor/co-worker isn't on your social network, you're sorely mistaken. Also, you might have invited them as a friend (along with the 507 other people) and forgot. So go beat your pillow or something but don't air your frustrations on a social network! Dummy! Here's the deal. If this is your venue to vent, fine. Don't give exact locations, names and circumstances. Vent enough that you will feel better, but make it vague enough that the person you're talking about won't be able to figure it out. Fair enough?

There are certain things that **CAN BE POSTED** to your wall: things you want everyone and their dog to see. Okay? Make sure you would feel okay with your Mom/boss/future husband/current wife reading. Then decide if you need to buy a diary. Remember you can also control who posts things (or pictures) to your wall or profile. The 'profile settings' tab should be your new best friend.

There are certain things that **SHOULD NOT BE POSTED** to your wall: party invites that are meant only for few select friends, leaving the rest of us out. Or party invites that are in another state—thanks!

Shameless self promotion. I don't like to talk to those people at parties, so it goes for on-line sites too. I want to hear about your accomplishments, but don't brag. There is a difference, it's a fine line I know, and sometimes you don't mean to brag, but it comes across that way. It bugs me bad. So proof read it a couple of times before you post. That way you can get the 'feel' of it before anybody reads it.

Now this is going to sound completely mean. Don't post your suicide note. If I see one more of those, I'm calling the cops! And if it's a false alarm, I will find you and beat the living crap out of you for scaring me. Call your pastor for God's sake.

Parent! Sibling! Or a REAL friend. A friend that you can trust to help you. I know you have one!

Please don't forward **CHAIN LETTER's**! If one more person tells me I'm going to die in the next five minutes, have bad luck all day, or be 'sorry' I didn't forward this on, I'm gonna FLIP OUT! The one that really get me…it's my Christian Duty to forward this message on and if I really cared about my friends I would….JUST SAY NO.

Chapter 8

Tests, Surveys, Groups & Gifts…Oh My!

I do caution you on the Tests! I took an IQ test while I was writing this book and failed poorly. Then my IQ level was displayed for everyone to laugh at. The part that really got me was that I had to enter my cell phone number in order to receive my results. Then I received at least seven text messages, in one minute intervals, asking me to sign up for various mindless things. That part was a bummer.

I later took another test in order to discover what kind of shoe fit my personality (I turned out to be a leopard skin spiked heel pump—whooo weee!), that was fun and I liked the outcome. You can make cartoon characterizations of yourself. You can become a 'fan' of anything. I've seen "I'm a fan of boobs" all the way to the Denver Nuggets (which I'm one of the fickle fans. You know, I only like them when they are doing well. Hey, at least I'm honest). There is something for everyone.

There are some very interesting groups on social networks. The number of groups will blow your mind. Not only can you search something like, 'Entertainment', but then you get a zillion sub-groups to check out under that. I've seen everything from I LOVE MARTINI'S to ALCOHOLICS ANONYMOUS. I've seen job hunters and recruiters to like-minded colleagues on Twitter. There are million different groups that might interest you. I joined an "Aspiring Authors" group on Facebook (I know, boring). I did find it interesting that I had the opportunity to help other authors with 'writers block'—if I knew how! There was the occasional writer promoting their new book. It was also helpful to find people offering their editing services. So that was pretty cool. However, some of these groups are just plain silly, so use at your own risk and comedic level.

I sent a LotaBurger, fries and a drink from New Mexico to my husband. It was a picture of the exact replica of their version of a 'happy meal'. He and I used to eat those all the time, and it was kinda cute. Why? How the hell do I know? It just seemed fun at the time.

I'm telling ya…sometimes there is no reason to the stuff you do on these social sites. I'm just warning you, okay? You can get stuck sending and receiving hugs and kisses, drinks and food. You can get stuck reading what everyone is doing, looking at pictures, taking stupid quizzes and aimlessly wandering around. I get invited to a million new applications each week and receiving gifts. Plus, you can forward these things on into oblivion. AWWWW! I've warned you. You have been warned!

DO NOT: do what I do sometimes: Facebook binge. The act of going on Facebook 'just for a sec' and suddenly finding that I have wasted 4 hours, and can't tell you where the afternoon went!

DO NOT: do what I do sometimes also: MySpace spiral. Start looking at one persons picture get distracted by their friend's photo, then I proceed to their site. Continue visiting their friend's pictures and what not, ending up forgetting where I started. Whew. What was I supposed to be doing? I'm sure this happens to everyone, and I'm just saying that a lot of time can be lost. I'm sure this is the whole idea of these sites, but man, can you loose yourself in there!

Chapter 9

Bad Grammar, Bad Spelling & Just Plain Bad

Okay, I'm not an English teacher. But this has got to stop! These are rules that first grader's know. Here is a refresher course for the few of you that have forgotten:

Your: adj., relating to you or yourself.
You're: is a contraction for You Are.
There: adv., in, at, or to that place.
Their: adj., relating to them.
They're: is another contraction, but it's for They Are

I vote for on-line social sites to add "spell check" to their sites. Agree? If you read younger generation posts, you will need the dictionary in the back of this book. I'm not kidding. It's a foreign language. There is no way I could translate everything, but I tried to include some interesting and funny things I found out about.

PLEASE: don't use bad language! Some of the girls I've seen (well, read) talk like sailors. I mean really. Must you? And the guys! Wow! I'm blushing right now remembering some of the postings I've read-and they are my friends! JK! Seriously though, show a little restraint even if it's only to impress your soon-to-be girlfriend's parents. We are looking up potential dates on social sites. You think I'm kidding….I'm watching you! The really funny thing is as I'm translating all the slang, which doesn't sound bad at first read, as I figure out what they are taking about I completely freak out. I'm not joshin' some of this stuff is really super duper nasty. Just so ya know.

Chapter 10

Incredible Stuff That Blows My Mind

In January of 2009 I read that MySpace is launching MySpace TV. They're hoping to lure amateur video makers to display their work. They will also 'rank' videos based on popularity. They will be in direct competition with YouTube.

Facebook recently spawned a new Boy Band. It's a group of classical musicians, a quartet, in Brittan. All the members met on Facebook and shared a love of music. They have signed a record deal with Universal. They even found a manager through Facebook. Many music acts have been launched on MySpace, but this was the first for Facebook.

There is also a Catholic Archbishop in Naples, Italy that enjoys using Facebook. He communicates with people all over the world. He's 65 years old.

If you are curious about how much time you spend on Twitter, you can go to twitterstats.com and they will graph out your time spent. Just plug in your username and it will generate a graph that records how many tweets you produce each hour, each day or each month. They claim over a 100,000 users right now.

The media has been up in arms lately because it seems as though "Citizen Journalists" are getting the scoop on stories before media journalists do. Citizen Journalists are people who capture video on their cell phones and/or post a story on Twitter before the regular TV media can get it on television. I'm not sure that being in the right place at the right time would classify a person as a 'journalist'. In the same sense, I wrote a book, does that really make me a writer? Probably not. I still find myself depending on the news or the newspaper for the latest scoop. However, the younger generation depends on the internet for their news. I've also noticed that my local TV stations are on Facebook and Twitter watching for stories and asking for ideas. I am the first to admit I heard about Michael Jackson's death when I logged on to my computer, I didn't have my television on at the time. What a trip!

YouTube is another interesting site. It's pretty self explanatory so I didn't include a lot of information here in the book. It's a video sharing website on which users can upload and share videos. My kids use it to watch music videos and find song lyrics. Before they buy a song on iTunes they will watch the music video to make sure they like the song. I like it because I can print out the song lyrics and freak out about what they are listening to. You can find a video upload to just about anything you want. My nephew has a couple of really cool skateboarding videos on YouTube. I uploaded one of my interviews on cell phone etiquette. I got depressed when I found out they post how many times your video has been viewed—mine wasn't a big hit (go figure). Well, hey when you compare it to a FRED video that gets about a million hits a day anybody would get bummed. Oh well, its still pretty cool that a person can share that kind of stuff.

Chapter 11

Dictionary, Terminology, Interpretations and Huh?

Most of the things said on these sites are far beyond my scope of understanding. The slang will make you rip your hair out. Just say it! What are these young people talking about?! So if you are like me, I've included **some** popular terminology that will help you (and me) better understand what the heck everyone is saying. Plus, most of these words are interchangeable within ALL the networking/social sites. Please don't judge me, I'm just the messenger here!

FACEBOOK:

Facebook Addict: Noun. (a.k.a. Facebook slut) who spends more time on face book making "friends" instead of spending time in the real word interacting with their real life friends.

Facebook Aim: using the Facebook wall to "instant message" in place of instant messenger or other such instant messaging programs.

Facebook Attack: When someone leaves their Facebook logged on and unattended and another person uses this opportunity to post a wall message. (An embarrassing joke, funny post or disgusting picture).

Facebook Baby: the product or a Facebook rumor concerning two people messaging often, leading to suspicion that they are dating or messaging so often they are going to have a Facebook baby.

Facebook Binge: (a.k.a. Blackout) Occurs when 'quickly checking Facebook' is used as a break in studying/tidying/working or other necessary but dull tasks that leads to a large amount of time missing from your day.

Facebook Bodycheck: a feeling of sadness/despair after checking one's Facebook wall and realizing that no one has responded to your posts.

Facebook Bomber: Someone who sends you many invitations a day for new groups, new applications, tags etc.

Facebook Boyfriend: A guy on your Facebook friends list that you add as your 'boyfriend'. Usually a joke put up by a single girl (or single guy). It makes one look like he/she is socially competent enough to actually have a steady relationship. This person is *not* their boyfriend in real life.

Facebook Breakup: A method of breaking up with your significant other through the Facebook private messaging system. This method of breaking up is considered the lowest of the low.

Facebook Buddy: A Facebook buddy is someone whom you've added as a friend on the website and when in conversation, one will say that he or she is a friend; when actuality a Facebook buddy is someone who you would never invite to your house.

Facebook Chameleon: Someone who frequently changes his or her profile picture on Facebook.

Facebook Chat: The newest and most convenient replacement for standard instant messaging of the past. Used to chat with other Facebook friends live. However, seems to have many glitches and users complain about it a lot.

Facebook Chat Rape: the act of leaving one word or offensive messages on a friends Facebook chat right before you log out, leaving them hanging, with no ability to respond or get the last word in.

Facebook Cheat: A person who makes a second or third Facebook profile just to improve his or her status in an application.

Facebook Chicken: When two people would like to add each other as friends, but don't want to be the one who make the friend invitation. This puts them in a game of Facebook Chicken, where they wait until the first person gives in to making the first add invitation. Silly!

Facebook Cock Block: When a girl or guy posts your Facebook with comments that make it appear as if the two of you are dating. This usually happens whenever your relational status is set to single (or in some cases when you don't have a relationship status set). By doing this, she effectively sends a nonverbal signal to potential mates that you are already dating, but haven't made it "official" yet.

Facebook Cool: Facebook cool means you are friends with people you don't even know.

Facebook Crawling: Aimless wandering through pages to see what's new and interesting.

Facebook Creeper: It's stalking for the online generation.

Facebook Crush: Is characterized by the unexplainable urge to revisit the friend's Photos tab repeatedly and checking to see if other friends have written new messages on their Wall. Spending long periods of time viewing their pictures. Usually afflicts users who are only somewhat acquainted.

Facebook Defense: After a friend takes embarrassing photos of you, staying logged into Facebook awaiting aforementioned "friend" to tag said photos of you, allowing you to quickly de-tag them before the rest of the world finds out.

Facebook Denial: When you wrongfully accuse others of being addicted to Facebook or stalking friends online when, in actuality, you are the one who is an addicted stalker.

Facebook Disease: When your profile picture doesn't look like you and it looks worse than what you look like in real life. (Can also apply to MySpace).

Facebook Divorce: When your spouse deletes you as a friend on Facebook.

Facebook Dump: When someone dumps their significant other by changing their Facebook relationship status instead of actually saying anything. Mean!

Facebook Effect: The feeling of déjà vu one often experiences upon meeting someone in real life then realizes they are already friends on Facebook.

Facebook Envy: The feeling you get when you come across an old friend on Facebook and realize that their life turned out way better and is more interesting than yours.

Facebook Escalation: When someone posts something to their Facebook status that causes such a commotion friends feel it necessary to seek out the poster by other means such as IM or even a phone call to get details.

Facebook Faceoff: After two people meet, the first person to add the other person as a friend on Facebook has lost the Facebook faceoff. The end result of 'chicken'.

Facebook Fakeout or Flop: one who puts a misleading picture of themselves on their page. (Usually to make themselves look better than they do in person).

Facebook Fatigue: The condition of being bored with Facebook.

Facebook Felony: Any embarrassing act that should have been kept secret, but somehow managed to be exposed via an incriminating Facebook photo album or News Feed item.

Facebook Foreplay: Writing increasingly sexy messages back and forth using Facebook.

Facebook Friend: someone you met and know in real life, but contact is confined to Facebook for reasons other than distance. Can also be someone you have never met.

Facebook Gold: The perfect Facebook picture. You look good at the same time doing something totally cool.

Facebook Grooming: To use Facebook chat/wall posts/ inbox messaging to get to know someone, in order to groom them, as so next time you see them out, the flirting has already begun.

Facebook Group: The making of a 'group' that anyone can join to discuss anything you deem is important enough to talk about or have in common.

Facebook Hang-Up: No, you haven't lost your

connection. Whomever you were chatting with decides to end the conversation without saying good bye! Hate that.

Facebook Hemorrhoid: The red swelling you get on your butt from sitting on the chair too long waiting for someone to comment on your Facebook wall. Happen to you yet?

Facebook Lesbian: A female on Facebook who lists herself as being in a relationship with another female friend. In reality she is heterosexual and lists the relationship out of some bizarre feminine vanity or to look cool. It's totally cool to be scandalous.

Facebook Limbo: You get a friends request on Facebook, if you want to, you can refrain from either accepting or rejecting the request, instead keep them hanging. Usually done 1) if you do not want to be friends with them, but it might cause trouble if you rejected them (they are a relative or something) or 2) if they already friended (acceptable word) you a few times and you rejected them, yet they can't take a hint.

Facebook Material: Usually a picture that is taken, reviewed, and agreed upon by all your friends as being Facebook worthy. Ask yourself, is this Facebook Material? *Should* this be Facebook material?

Facebook Memory: The act of using Facebook to recall a previous night's intoxicated/drug induced event using photos added by others because you have no personal memory. I remember those days (well, without the drug part, drinking yes, drugs no. Am I rambling?)

Facebook News Feed: This feature lets people know when you drop, add or create a group, become friends with someone they don't know, and even lets people know the change in any status, be it relationship or otherwise.

Facebook Ninja: A person appearing in Facebook messages or pictures without owning an account. A Facebook Ninja can never be "tagged" and never appears on a wall. Therefore, they never need their own personal account; they can 'visit' vicariously through other people's accounts.

Facebook Official: The ultimate definition of a relationship—when on one's Facebook profile it says "In a Relationship" and your significant other's name. It's official now.

Facebook Out: A person listing his or herself as gay/lesbian but hasn't told anyone in real life.

Facebook Paparazzi: When someone takes photos of embarrassing moments or things you probably shouldn't be doing, then uploads and tags them on Facebook for all to see. Kind of like the *real* paparazzi. Have you ever had the paparazzi follow you? Me neither, but I can imagine.

Facebook Party: A large number of people log on to Facebook. Usually done at LAN parties or during class while students are bored.

Facebook Porn: Defined as those rather questionable pictures posted while wearing skimpy clothes/bathing suits and posing in sexual positions. These photos conform to Facebook 'terms of use' rules therefore they are not deleted.

Facebook Pull: The act of copying photos from an individual's Facebook page to your computer.

Facebook Purgatory: If you get a friends request on Facebook and you do not accept or reject it for an extended period of time. This interim time period is call Facebook purgatory. Note that this is not the same as Limbo; purgatory is temporary (the person might be cool) and limbo is permanent.

Facebook Quote: When someone says something foolish, stupid, or of very little value that is then added as a 'Facebook book quote' on Facebook so the whole world can admire their stupidity.

Facebook Rage: When a person gets angry at another person for interrupting their Facebook time. You have got to be kidding! It's not like you are in the middle of a massage! (or were you? Ew!)

Facebook Reveal: Spending time in someone's profile allows you to deduce the *real* them.

Facebook Scum: Advertisements listed in the margins of Facebook. I guess this is annoying to some people.

Facebook Slam: The act of denying a friend request. It can also be used in the past-tense form, 'Facebook slammed.'

Facebook Status: You write about what you are currently doing or your current relationship.

Facebook Suicide: The act of de-activating or disconnecting from the virtual world to reconnect with the real world. Something I need to do.

Facebook Sympathy: Changing your status on Facebook in such a way as to attract sympathy messages from your friends.

Facebook Tag: The act of identifying people in your photos by naming the faces found in the images.

Facebook Tripping: Happens when you develop a crush on someone from browsing their Facebook profile or pictures. Usually someone you don't know or never met.

Facebook Trolling: The act of scrolling through other people's "friend list", looking for anyone you knows that you can "friend" for yourself.

Facebook Twit: posting the same status on both Twitter and Facebook at the same time.

Facebook Value: A concept where the value of an activity/picture/event is measured in the potential attention it will get on Facebook. High or Low value.

Facebook Vulture: One who will contact an attractive male or female friend on Facebook within the first few weeks of the victim's relationship status change from "In A Relationship with…" to "Single". Best done within the private message, but the vultures will use wall posts instead. It gives them the creeper factor.

MYSPACE:

MySpace Addict: A MySpace addict is a person who is on MySpace 24/7 and is always finding new and cool MySpace layouts. Usually has a custom MySpace that looks more like a website. This person may have a lot of friends and gets professional pictures done of themselves.

MySpace Angle: When the camera is placed above your head at an angle to take a MySpace picture, usually done by yourself.

MySpace Arrest: When your account is deleted by the MySpace police (Tom Anderson, President).

MySpace Banger: a person who posts racial slurs against dangerous gangs or people. Just asking for trouble while in the safety of their own home.

MySpace Bankruptcy: loosing your password and having to start all over again.

MySpace Booty: Searching and finding people of the opposite sex to hook up with. You can perform searches within a 5-10 mile radius of your location if you like.

MySpace Bulletin: A group of words posted for all of your MySpace friends to see that typically consists of a curse of bad luck, survey, pleas for comments; insane obnoxious list of things wanted in a relationship usually includes some sappy love story, announcement of new pictures, etc.

MySpace Comeback: Deleting your old MySpace and returning with a brand spanking new one.

MySpace (comment) Tennis: When you're reading part of a conversation between two people that sparks your interest, and you decide you just HAVE to read the other part of the conversation. Then you go to the other person's page, and find yourself going back and forth from page to page following the conversation. Private profiles prevent MySpace Comment Tennis from happening.

MySpace Crash: When a profile is so overloaded with items, applications, videos, etc., that when the page is attempted to be viewed, that it either takes an excruciatingly long time, or it won't load, or it will just crash your internet connection.

MySpace Deceiving Default: It's considered a 'trick' where a person's picture makes them look totally hot and when you lurk the rest of their pictures, turns out it's not the same person.

MySpace Detective: a person who can find out all sorts of information about you. They seem to be 'blessed' in the area of detective work and snooping out information.

MySpace Drama: pointless acts of back-stabbing, insulting and general hurtful conversation about other people.

MySpace Escapee: a person who has deleted their MySpace account and feels a sense of improved life due to this decision.

MySpace Flu: (a.k.a. HIV) considered a sickness of never leaving your house because you are stuck on MySpace all the time.

MySpace Forums: areas where you can discuss any imaginable topic. Mostly viewed as 'stupid' by MySpace users, but seem to be very popular just the same.

MySpace Hair: a hairstyle that is ratty, messy and over-all terrible. It's supposed to look like that-and no, I didn't make this up!

MySpace Hopping: moving from one MySpace to another and back again. Over and over.

MySpace Individual: someone who copies 'individual' thoughts or ideas from another person and tries to pass them off as their own ideas.

MySpace Investigation: looking at someone's MySpace to find out more about them.

MySpace It Up: putting random pictures on MySpace. Or anything special enough you feel the need to 'MySpace it up' or Post it on your page.

MySpace Jackin: yes, you guessed it, pleasuring yourself to pictures posted on sites.

MySpace Lag: when MySpace is experiencing technical difficulties and it takes forever to load pictures or various items on a page.

MySpace Layout: The MySpace layout is basically the page design of your account. The layout determines how your account page looks and where different links and profiles are located on the page. There are many different MySpace layouts available all over the web. Some layouts are given to you for free and some are not free. (When you choose a layout on the web they will give you the code of that specific layout. All you have to do then is type that code into your profile box at the bottom of your MySpace page and it will upload).

MySpace Loner: A person who has a lot of MySpace friends, but doesn't have very many friends in real life.

MySpace Love: waiting for hours to get a comment from your MySpace crush.

Lurk: someone who spends lots of time on other peoples MySpace but doesn't leave any clue they were there. This person seems to know information about you without you telling him directly.

Marketing: having your top friends to post comments about you in order to make another person jealous.

MySpace Meow: a cat that has a MySpace account.

MySpace Mom: A woman over the age of 40 who gets a MySpace account to either re-live their teenage years or to spy on her kids. Usually tries to make friends with her children's friends. (I *may* unfortunately fall into this category—how sad am I?).

MySpace Monkey: a person who uses a public computer (Library, café) to get on MySpace.

MySpace Muscles: Are achieved through MySpace in the comfort of your own home without the fear of any consequences coming from your trash-talking.

MySpace Name: nick-name used on MySpace.

MySpace Noise: A derogatory term directed at bands/ music artists that have become popular through MySpace.

MySpace Nude: pictures that conform to the 'terms of use' under MySpace rules, but are still pretty dirty in my opinion.

MySpace PDA: 'public display of affection'. Used to describe a person who posts comments or pictures about their Boy/Girl Friend only.

MySpace Phonebook: a school yearbook used to find more people to invite as your friends.

Pwn'd: This is actually pretty funny. This word was originally 'owned' which was used to describe the level of a beating a person received. Then, someone *accidently* typed pwn'd. The typo stuck. Go figure.

MySpace Raid: when a school punishes actions performed or pictures posted on MySpace by their students.

MySpace Rush-Hour: usually the time right after school that the most kids are logged on at the same time.

MySpace Spiral: A situation in which one intends on viewing a single profile on MySpace but views that individuals intriguing friends, which forces one to investigate said profiles until one forgets where they started in the first place.

Spyspacing: the act of spying on the guys or girls that you are dating. **Spyspacing** allows you to see if you are being spaceplayed. Finding out if the stories you are being told are true.

MySpace Talk: Writing as if you are on speed. Using a lot of "quotation marks", explanation points and lots of periods!!!! Okay????? :0)!! Do you know what I'm *&%__@$# talking about???

MySpace Thug: a person that threatens another on MySpace but usually doesn't act on their threats in real life. Usually a big talker, no action. A bully type.

MySpace V-Card: a person that doesn't have any comments on their MySpace (a virgin).

MySpace Waiting Period: a three day period people wait to add people they just met to their MySpace friends.

TWITTER:

Twitter Douche: An addicted Twitter user who posts every single thing that happens to them every few moments.

Twitter Head: A twitter head is a person who likes to twitter 24 hours a day, 7 days a week. They will twitter about anything that comes to mind. Even twittering about twittering.

Twitter Lambs: Celebrities have a swarm of followers which are referred to as "Twitter Lambs" that respond to every update they receive via SMS, online or by cell phone. Each "Twitter Lamb" then re-tweets "RT" their thoughts to the sender.

Twitter Life: a person who is so caught up in twittering their lives that they miss the party because they are in the corner twittering what's going on.

Twitter Litter: Tweeting things that nobody cares about. The doo doo the kitty left in the box.

Twitter MILF: an amazing woman and **M**om **I**'d **L**ike to **F**ollow.

Twitter Novel: using 5 or 6 tweets to write a super long message. Ignoring the fact that twitter was made for 140 characters only.

Twitter Points: the number of friends you have. Usually not used as a compliment. You can loose your points for doing something bad.

Twitter Quitter: person who deletes their twitter account.

Twitter Twat: someone who has zero followers.

Twitterable: something worthy of being twittered.

Twitterazti: stalkers that follow strangers on Twitter.

Twitterbang: to simulate sex in 140 characters or less.

Twitterdict: a Twitter addict.

Twitterfare: an affair between two people on Twitter.

Twittergrounded: When a person uses the post and reply features so much within a short period of time, the service temporarily shuts down their tweeting privileges.

Twitterism: deep insights about life that are 140 characters or less. Immediately quoted by others and made popular.

Twitterjam: trouble accessing Twitter due to lots of people logged on.

Twittermock: making fun of someone because they use Twitter instead of Facebook or MySpace.

Twitterpaited: Having a huge crush on someone. By the way, my good friend Rachelle used this word WAY before Twitter did, just so you know.

Twitterpanions: People that you communicate with primarily via Twitter. They can be your followers, people you follow, etc.

Twitterpedia: The act of using Twitter to receive answers to a question from friends rather than looking it up yourself.

Twitterpimp: Someone who introduces you to Twitter. They recruit friends, family members, and strangers to join the addiction of 140 characters. Before meeting them your life was Twitter-free.

Twittervention: The act of confronting someone who goes overboard with their status updates on social networking sites such as Facebook and MySpace, when it would be more appropriate to use a social messaging site such as twitter, or a blog.

Twitterville: Your group of Twitter followers that one particularly likes to chat with. Twitter favorites, friends, followers, and fans. Your own town of people.

Twitterquette: The unwritten laws of the acceptable and polite use of Twitter. Talk about **something** not just anything. No, I didn't add this word myself!